Contents

Introduction

In this book we look at photographs and other kinds of images of schools, from Victorian times up until the 1960s. We examine these images for clues about the past and see what we can learn from them about the way people used to be educated. On pages 30-31, you can find some questions and points to explore, to encourage further discussion of the pictures.

1853

← This is a school for very poor children.

↑ Ragged schools were set up in the 19th century to teach poor children from inner cities. The children were taught reading, writing and arithmetic, as well as practical skills. They were given food, clothing and a place to stay.

PAST IN PICTURES

A photographic view of
Schools

Published in paperback in 2014 by Wayland
Copyright © Wayland 2014

Wayland
338 Euston Road
London NW1 3BH

Wayland Australia
Level 17/207 Kent Street
Sydney, NSW 2000

Editor: Joyce Bentley
Concept Design: Lisa Peacock
Designer: Elaine Wilkinson
Researchers: Laura Simpson and Hester Vaizey
at The National Archives

Picture acknowledgements: Material reproduced by
courtesy of The National Archives, London, England.
www.nationalarchives.gov.uk.
Catalogue references and picture acknowledgements
Main cover: INF2/43 Bricked up windows in a
wartime school 1940s, INF9/1007 Prep room., St.
Catherine's School, Bramley, Surrey 1930s, INF9/448
Rugby School, Chemistry laboratory, 1926-1948,
INF2/43 f1938 Toys in nursery class at a Junior
School in Holloway,1939-1945, back cover: r INF
2/1 Children's nursery, 1941, l COPY1/555/200
Elementary Art class at LCC School, Southampton
Row, London, title page: COPY1/422/372 Lavender
Hill Board School typewriting class, 1895, p2:
INF2/43 f1938 Toys in nursery class at a Junior
School in Holloway,1939-1945, p3: ED138/51 Children
from Trafford Road school, Salford, assemble for
evacuation, 1 September 1939, p4: ZPER34/23 (p520)
Brook Street Ragged School, 1853, p5: ZPER34/56
(P 349) Illustrated London News, New School Room,
Boy's Home, Regent's Park Road, 1870, p6: ZPER35/2
Children sifting dust in an brickyard, 1871, p7:
COPY1/373 ii (9) A Dame School PH Emerson 1885,
p8: COPY1/382 Schoolchildren playing marbles,
1887, p9: COPY1/422/372 Lavender Hill Board
School typewriting class, 1895, p10: COPY1/160
Music class, Milton Board School 1900, p11:
COPY1/160 PE class at Milton Board School, 1900,
p12: Copy1/168/213, p13: COPY1/491/104 Tennis in
the grounds of Knowle Hall School, Bournemouth,
1905, p14: COPY1/481 Children on the steps of
the Charles Thompson Poor Children's Mission,
Birkenhead,1905, p15: COPY1/555/200 Elementary
Art class at LCC School, Southampton Row, London,
1911, p16: INF9/1007 Prep room., St. Catherine's
School, Bramley, Surrey 1930s, p17:, INF9/426
Westminster School class 1930s, p18: INF9/501 Class
at Wycombe Abbey school 1930s, p19: INF9/448
Rugby School, Chemistry laboratory, 1926-1948,
p20: ED138/51 Children from Trafford Road school,
Salford, assemble for evacuation, 1 September 1939,
p21: INF 2/1 Children's nursery, 1941, p22: INF2/1
Air Training Corps school unit, 1941, p23: INF13/144
f23 Make Do And Mend, Reinforce Children's Clothes
poster,1939-1945, p24: INF14/13 Home Front
Children learning to 'Dig for Victory', p25: INF2/43
Bricked up windows in a wartime school 1940s,
p26: INF3/210 Weapons From Scrap Metal, School
Scrap Metal Dump, p27: INF2/44 f2335 Pooles Park
school, North London PT lesson1944, p28: INF2/43
f1938 Toys in nursery class at a Junior School in
Holloway,1939-1945, p29: Landskrona Museum / IBL
/ Mary Evans

A cataloguing record for this title is available at the
British Library.
Dewey number: 371

ISBN: 978 0 7502 8338 0

Printed in China
10 9 8 7 6 5 4 3 2 1

Wayland is a division of Hachette Children's Books,
an Hachette UK company
www.hachette.co.uk

↓ **This boys' school was set up to stop children from becoming criminals.**

↑ This school in London was called the Boys' Home. The school's owners took poor children, who they thought were in danger of turning to a life of crime, and taught them how to read and write. They also taught them trades such as carpentry, tailoring and shoemaking.

← In Victorian times, many children did not go to school.

← These girls are sifting dust in a brickyard. The dust is mixed with clay to make bricks. Up to 30,000 children aged 5 to 16 worked in British brickyards. This began to change in the 1870s when education became compulsory.

↓ **This school is in the teacher's home.**

↑ This type of primary school was called a dame school. They were popular from the 17th to the 19th century. The teacher was usually an elderly woman who ran the school in her home. This dame school is being taught by a fisherman's wife in East Anglia.

↓ The children in this school yard are playing marbles.

↑ Children in Victorian times loved playing outdoor games. As well as marbles, popular games included blindman's buff, hide-and-seek and hopscotch. These games didn't need much equipment and could be played in any open space, be it the school yard or the street.

⬇ **These girls are learning to use a typewriter.**

↑ The typewriter was invented in 1874. By the 1890s, typewriters were a common sight in offices. Most typists were women. In some schools, girls were taught how to type. This was seen as a useful skill for their working lives.

↓ **These schoolgirls are learning how to play musical instruments.**

↑ Female students in this class are learning to play two different kinds of stringed instrument: the lute and the violin. In the 19th and early 20th century girls from wealthy families were often taught skills like music and sewing, as well as reading, writing and arithmetic.

These boys from
a boarding school
are being taught P.E.

↑ Like today, schools in the 1900s viewed physical education (P.E.) as a vital part of the school curriculum. In those days it was called physical culture. Boys were also taught combat sports such as boxing, wrestling and fencing.

↓ This poster shows scenes from a school day.

↑ Here we can see some examples of early 20th-century school life. In the left-hand picture, a boy is being punished by having to wear a dunce's cap. Discipline in schools could be very harsh. Children were often beaten with a cane on the hand or bottom. Another punishment was writing 'lines'. This meant writing out the same sentence a hundred times or more.

1905

↓ At this school in Bournemouth, some girls are playing tennis.

↑ Knole Hall was a private school where wealthy parents could send their daughters. Notice that the girls are playing tennis in long skirts and there are no court markings. Tennis was very different in those days! By the early 1900s, there were a number of independent girls' schools. They taught their students how to be good housewives, but also subjects like geography, history and grammar.

↓ Poor children were sometimes looked after by charities.

↑ Some of the children living at Charles Thompson's Poor Children's Mission in Birkenhead. Thompson opened his mission in 1892. He fed and clothed the children, educated them, gave them toys and took them on outings.

⬇ These schoolgirls are learning to draw by copying the pictures on the blackboard.

↑ This is an art class at a London school. The girls are wearing smocks to protect their smart clothes. The focus of art lessons was on learning to draw exactly what you see. Students were discouraged from using their imaginations or being creative.

↓ **Schoolgirls are writing and reading.**

↑ These students attend an independent girls' school in Surrey. They wrote in exercise books with steel-nibbed pens and ink. Teachers were very strict and students were sometimes beaten. Girls were caned more rarely than boys, and nearly always on the palm of the hand. Other punishments included having to learn French verbs, or being forced to return to school on Saturday morning for 'detention'.

↓ The schoolboys in this classroom are sitting in rows working hard.

↑ The pupils are all boys. Mixed-gender schools began in the 19th century, but did not become common until the 1950s. The pupils are seated in rows facing the front. Each pupil has his own desk. The desks have sloping, flip-top lids.

⬇ This is a woodwork class. The girls are busy making things.

↑ These girls are making furniture and other wooden items.
There are no power tools in this workshop. The girl on the
left is using a foot-powered saw to cut the wood.

↓ These schoolboys are doing experiments.

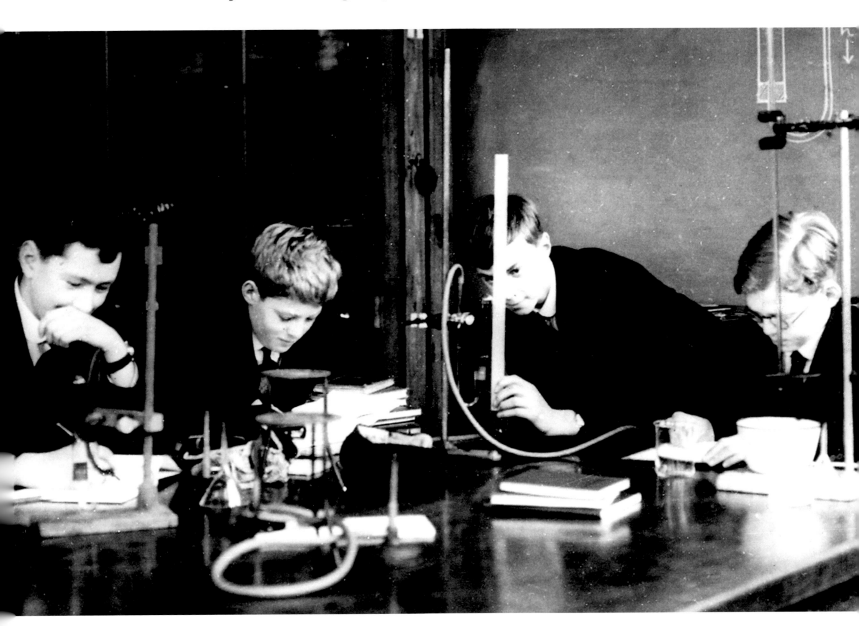

↑ In most classes, students would be seated at desks, copying off a blackboard.
Chemistry lessons gave children a rare opportunity to learn for themselves
by carrying out practical experiments.

⬇ **When war broke out, children were evacuated from their homes.**

↑ In September 1939, World War II began. The government feared that cities would be bombed. Millions of city children were sent to live in the countryside. They had to get used to a new home, a new school and life without their parents.

↓ The children in this nursery are playing outside.
One boy is driving a toy tractor.

↑ Before the 1940s, most young children stayed with their mothers at home.
During World War II, things started to change. Many fathers had to go
and fight, and mothers were encouraged to work. As a result, many more
chidren went to nursery.

⬇ These schoolboys have joined an organisation called the Air Training Corps.

↑ The Air Training Corps was set up in 1941. Its aim was to prepare boys of 13 and upwards for entry into the Royal Air Force (RAF). The boys were called cadets. These cadets are being inspected by an RAF officer.

← This poster is telling mothers to strengthen their children's clothes so they last longer.

← During World War II, clothes were in short supply. Clothing was rationed, meaning that people could only buy a limited amount. By making clothes last longer, people would not need to buy so much. This was called 'Make Do and Mend'.

↓ These children are being taught how to grow vegetables.

↑ Food was rationed during World War II. A campaign called 'Dig For Victory' encouraged people to grow their own food. Schools became actively involved in the campaign, and many had vegetable plots in their grounds.

⬇ **In this classroom the windows have been bricked up.**

⬆ During World War II, many schools had a refuge room where staff and children could go during an air raid. The walls were lined with sandbags to muffle the blast. The windows were bricked up because of the threat of flying glass.

⬇ This poster is telling people to save scrap metal.

⬆ During World War II, the government was short of metal to build weapons and war machines. Some schools had a scrap metal dump where children could deposit any metal items they no longer needed. These could be used to help the war effort.

↓ The boys in this playground are having a P.E. lesson.

↑ This scene in a North London school seems to show life continuing as normal, despite the war. However, in the year this picture was taken, this school suffered bomb damage, one of its pupils died and several were made homeless in air raids.

⬇ At nursery school, children liked to play with toys.

⬆ In this nursery school in London, children are playing with a rocking horse and a handcart. Rocking horses were popular toys from the 17th to the mid-20th century.

↓ Schoolchildren rinse their teeth with fluoride.

↑ In the 1960s, the government tried to fight tooth decay in children by getting schools to give their pupils fluoride mouth rinses. Fluoride is a chemical that protects teeth from decay. The children were given the mouth rinse once a week and asked to hold it in their mouths for 60 seconds.

Questions to Ask and Points to Explore

Picture on page 4

Questions to ask

1. Why do you think the children are learning practical skills?

2. Why did the teacher put up a sign saying 'Thou shalt not steal'?

Points to explore

Room: materials, decoration, messiness, crowdedness, lighting
People: clothes, tools, activities
Equipment: names, function, materials

Picture on page 5

Questions to ask

1. Why might all the children be dressed similarly?

2. What sort of lesson do you think they're having?

Points to explore

Room: size, decoration, crowdedness
People: clothes, age, poses, behaviour

Picture on page 6

Questions to ask

1. Why are the children barefoot?

2. How do you think they feel about their job?

Points to explore

Background: building, state of repair, dirtiness
People: clothes, age, pose, mood

Picture on page 7

Questions to ask

1. Is this school well-equipped?

2. Is this a good or bad place for teaching and learning?

Points to explore

Background: furniture, setting, weather
People: clothes, age, gender

Picture on page 8

Questions to ask

1. How is this school yard different from modern playgrounds?

2. Why is there a circle in the dust?

3. What is the boy carrying on his back on the right of the picture?

Points to explore

Background: building, school yard, materials
People: age, gender, clothes, activities

Picture on page 9

Questions to ask

1. How could this classroom and its equipment be improved to make teaching and learning easier and more enjoyable?

2. Have you ever seen or used a typewriter?

3. Why aren't they used any more?

Points to explore

Room: furniture, fittings, decoration
People: age, gender, pose, mood, clothes, hairstyles

Picture on page 10

Questions to ask

1. Why do you think this might be a difficult class to teach?

2. Have you ever seen or heard a lute?

3. What modern instrument does it remind you of?

Points to explore

Background: building, materials, state of repair
People: age, gender, clothes

Picture on page 11

Questions to ask

1. How does this compare to a P.E. class in a modern school?

2. What are the disadvantages of doing P.E. in your school clothes?

Points to explore

Background: buildings, materials, season
People: gender, clothes, pose, size of class, behaviour

Picture on page 12

Questions to ask

1. How does the classroom scene in the middle picture differ from modern classrooms?

Points to explore

Typeface: readability, mood, purpose
People: clothes, feelings

Picture on page 13

Questions to ask

1. Why do you think it might have been difficult to play tennis in this way?

2. Why do you think this was a school for children of wealthy families?

3. Do the spectators seem interested in the match?

Points to explore

Background: building, setting, grass, benches
People: gender, age, clothing
Equipment: racket, net

Picture on page 14

Questions to ask

1. How can you tell these children are very poor?

2. What can you tell about their mood from their faces?

Points to explore

Background: building, street, cleanliness
People: age, gender, size, clothing, mood, cleanliness

Picture on page 15

Questions to ask

1. Looking carefully at the items in this room, what other subject do you think might be taught in here?

2. How does this compare to an art lesson in a modern school?

3. A couple of the girls in the back row are using quill pens. What were these made from?

Points to explore

Background: furniture, layout, decoration, objects, state of repair, lighting

Picture on page 16

Questions to ask

1. Can you guess what time of year it is?

2. What is in the metal pots on the table?

Points to explore

Room: furniture, decoration, fireplace
People: age, gender, uniforms, hairstyles

Picture on page 17

Questions to ask

1. How does this compare to a modern classroom?

2. Why do the desks have lids that open?

Points to explore

Room: furniture, windows, decoration
People: age, gender, clothing, hairstyles, mood, activity

Picture on page 18

Questions to ask

1. What do you think the girl on the right is making?

2. What is the name of the metal object attached to the side of the table in the foreground?

3. What is it used for?

Points to explore

Room: furniture, equipment, lighting
People: age, gender, clothing, hairstyles

Picture on page 19

Questions to ask

1. How does this room and its equipment differ from that found in the chemistry department of a modern school?

Points to explore

Room: furniture, materials, equipment, decoration
People: age, gender, mood, clothing, accessories

Picture on page 20

Questions to ask

1. Why do you think this photograph is so grainy?

2. Do the children look happy or sad to be going on a journey?

3. Why are they wearing labels around their necks?

Points to explore

People: age, clothing, mood

Picture on page 21

Questions to ask

1. What time of year do you think this is, and why?

2. Does this look like a clean, safe place for young children to play?

Points to explore

Background: building, play area, furniture, toys
People: age, clothing, mood

Picture on page 22

Questions to ask

1. Why do you think these cadets look keen to be part of the Air Training Corps?

2. Why do you think the government wanted to recruit boys to the RAF during this period?

Points to explore

Background: buildings
People: age, gender, clothing, mood

Picture on page 23

Questions to ask

1. Who do you think this poster was aimed at?

2. Why does it show women's hands mending the clothes, and not men's?

3. Do you think this poster does a good job of getting across its message?

Points to explore

Text: typography, art, design, message, historical context

Picture on page 24

Questions to ask

1. Why were there food shortages during World War II?

2. Can you identify any of the tools being used in this photograph?

Points to explore

Background: buildings, materials, allotments, equipment
People: age, gender, clothing

Picture on page 25

Questions to ask

1. Why do you think the teacher is putting pictures over the windows?

2. What do you think it would have been like having a lesson in this classroom?

Points to explore

Room: materials, lighting, window
People: age, gender, mood

Picture on page 26

Questions to ask

1. Do you think this poster gets its message across well?

2. Did you understand it the first time you looked at it?

3. Can you think of any ways to improve the poster so the message is clearer?

4. Why do you think it says 'ALL BOYS CAN HELP', not 'ALL CHILDREN CAN HELP'?

Points to explore

Text: typography, art, design, message, historical context

Picture on page 27

Questions to ask

1. What time of year do you think this photograph was taken, and why?

2. What do you think it would have been like going to school during wartime?

Points to explore

Background: building, materials, design
People: age, gender, clothing

Picture on page 28

Questions to ask

1. Why do you think rocking horses are not so popular today?

2. What is a handcart?

3. What were they used for?

Points to explore

Background: decoration, cleanliness, toys
People: age, clothing, hairstyles

Picture on page 29

Questions to ask

1. Do the children look like they are enjoying the mouth rinse?

2. Do you think that giving children the mouth rinse while they are in class is a good way of preventing tooth decay?

3. Why might this be better than giving it to parents to give to their children?

Points to explore

Room: posters, desks, decor
People: gender, clothing

Some suggested answers can be found on the Wayland website www.waylandbooks.co.uk.

Further Information

Books

At School *(What Was It Like In the Past)* by Louise and Richard Spilsbury (Heinemann Library, 2003)

Life At School *(Then and Now)* by Vicky Yates (Heinemann Library, 2008)

School *(History from Photographs)* by Kath Cox and Pat Hughes (Wayland, 2006)

Websites

http://www.nationalarchives.gov.uk/education/

http://www.bbc.co.uk/schools/primaryhistory/victorian_britain/children_at_school

http://www.bbc.co.uk/schools/primaryhistory/world_war2/

http://www.spartacus.schoolnet.co.uk/EDragged.htm

Glossary

air raid A bomb attack on a ground target carried out by aircraft.

boarding school A school where students live during term time.

brickyard A place where bricks are made.

charity An organisation set up to provide help for those in need.

compulsory Required by law.

curriculum The subjects that students must study while at school.

dame school A small primary school, usually run by an elderly woman from her own home.

dunce's cap A paper cone that students had to wear on their heads as a mark of disgrace.

evacuated Taken from a place of danger to a safe place.

fencing The sport of fighting with swords, known as foils.

housewife A woman who manages a home.

lute A stringed instrument that is plucked like a guitar. It has a long neck and a rounded body with a flat front.

mission An organisation, usually Christian, set up to help people.

mixed-gender school A school in which girls and boys are educated together.

private school A school that is supported by fees paid by the parents of students.

ragged school A school that offered free education to very poor children. Ragged schools flourished during the late 19th century.

rationing Allowing people only a limited amount of something, such as clothing or food, because of shortages.

Royal Air Force (RAF) The British air force, founded in 1918.

scrap metal Metal parts that are no longer needed.

smock A loose garment worn over one's clothes to protect them.

tailoring The craft of making clothes.

typewriter A machine with keys for producing letters and other characters on paper.